POETS FACING THE WALL

The Raving Press
Mission, Texas

Copyright © 2018 The Raving Press

All Rights Reserved.

ISBN-10: 0-9989965-5-6

ISBN-13: 978-0-9989965-5-4

Dedication

This anthology is dedicated to all Americans and people of the world who believe in freedom, democracy, diplomacy, and human rights.

Foreword

This anthology will be our first to include four different languages, and contributions by writers from as far as New Delhi, India, making this not just an international publication, but a global one.

Many of the works you will see in this anthology come from prize-winning authors, as well as from writers relatively new to the publishing process, but who exhibited a lot of heart and passion. And that is why we went to the poets primarily for this project.

It is the poets who speak from the heart. It is the poets who are historically willing to risk liberty, life, and limb to stand up for justice, for humanity in an inhumane phase of history, and for beauty in an otherwise savage world. Poetry may not bring riches. Poetry may not win wars. Poetry may not even sway the masses when the track that's been laid before them leads the train down a dark and irreversible path to their own destruction. But poets, as opposed to historians, politicians, media talking heads, and Monday-morning quarterbacks, call the plays as they should be in real time regardless of the fury and fire they may spark in those whose interest is to keep the people blind to the truth.

We hope that this project and future ones (here's wishing the First Amendment a very long life still) will inspire and fill with hope everyone who comes across it.

That they may sample the brilliance of the minds that contributed the sacred fruit of their ponderings to this publication and feel elevated. That they may repurpose the walls that ignorance and hate erect to divide people and use them as bridges on which all can walk in each other's shoes and see a common humanity.

Contents

Introduction **1**
An Inheritance of Fear **10**
As We Forgive Those **13**
Ave Blanca **14**
Blue Again **15**
Blues for Jose Antonio Elena Rodriguez **16**
Construction of First Border Wall Segment to Begin in a South Texas Wildlife Refuge **18**
The Difference Between Held and Held **21**
My Exit **23**
The Greatest, Most Beautiful Soliloquy EVER! **25**
Ten Commandments Updated **26**
Guardian of the Mountains **28**
I Am Chicano **30**
Liberty and the Pursuit of Happiness **37**
You Make the Call **39**
Myopia of Belonging **41**
Northward Bound **42**
Hacia El Norte **44**
Oh, Say Can You See **45**
On Day 1, We Will Being Working **46**
FRONTEXTO #98 **48**
FRONTEXTO #105 **50**
FRONTEXTO #139 **52**
FRONTEXTO #152 **54**
Border Crossings **56**

A Fluid Border **57**

Wide Open **59**

The Fool's Game **59**

Blurred Vision **59**

denizen z. two **60**

Blood, Sweat and Tears **62**

Conflict **64**

Survival **66**

Hollywood **68**

Musings **69**

Song for America XXIII (the nations's anthem) **71**

Song for America XXV **73**

Song for America XXVIII (for Marvin Gaye) **76**

De este lado del muro **78**

Rima infantil **79**

Ten Feet Higher **80**

The Promised Wall **81**

Shelter **82**

Closure **84**

more harm than good **86**

This Just In **88**

Walls Divide Us **90**

Mr. Trump Tear Down This Wall **91**

Walking Around **92**

"A, Homeboy" **93**

The Wall **95**

Lament for Emma Lazarus **96**

Ghost Wall **97**
Wall **98**
We are Sisters! **99**
Tinta Negra **102**
Black Ink **103**
Tinta Nera **104**
What I Need Now **105**
In Concert **106**
The Travel North **107**
Keep my dream Alive **108**
GRETEL **109**
WHERE HAVE ALL THE FLOWERS GONE **111**
CROSSINGS **113**
Nuestros Niños **115**
Δικά μας παιδιά. **117**
Our Sons and Daughters **119**
Contributor Bios **121**
About The Raving Press **138**

Introduction

by Hector Luis Alamo

"Good fences make good neighbours," goes the line by our national poet. But the Enlightenment thinker Jean-Jacques Rousseau, probing the source of social inequality, blamed the first person to invent walls and other boundaries as the true creator of society. "From how many crimes, wars and murders," he writes in 1754, "from how many horrors and misfortunes might not any one have saved mankind, by pulling up the stakes, or filling up the ditch, and crying to his fellows, 'Beware of listening to this impostor; you are undone if you once forget that the fruits of the earth belong to us all, and the earth itself to nobody.' "

Before the United States drew its line in the sand between it and Mexico and said "This is mine," what United Statesians obsessively refer to as *the border* was mostly desert, sectioned off by mountains, and carved across by two untamed rivers surging toward separate seas. The land was far from lifeless, however. When the conquistador Francisco Vázquez de Coronado set out across the future states of Arizona and New Mexico in 1540, rather than the cities of gold he had hoped to find, he met a chain of villages populated by indigenous peoples-- the Zuni, the Hopi, the Apache, and, most likely, the Navajo--who had learned to adapt to this unforgiving yet bountiful terrain. A decade earlier, a Spanish hidalgo by the name of Álvar Núñez Cabeza de Vaca, having survived a shipwreck off the western coast of La Florida, stumbled across the Karankawa and Coahuiltecan peoples of East Texas, immediately becoming their slave, and later their supposed healer. In 1680, in the New Spain province of

Santa Fe de Nuevo México, Pueblo Indians launched a rebellion against the Spanish colonizers, managing to regain control of their native lands (for a little while).

History is clear: The people were there before the border.

Napoleon's sale of Louisiana to the United States in 1803 marked the young empire's first border with what would soon become a newly independent Mexico. Both nations considered the land on either side of the Sabine River a backcountry, largely unexplored, still dominated by a few militant Indian tribes fiercely protecting their lands against any intrusion. Only the most freewheeling, intrepid Mexicans and United Statesians attempted to make their lives here, risking what little they had for a chance at bigger fortunes, or at least greater freedoms, than those available in the bustling commercial centers of Mexico City, Veracruz, New York City, and Charleston. Many were *rancheros*: retired soldiers and moneyed men granted plots of land by the Mexican government in its effort to settle the territory and finally bring the native peoples under control. But the frontiersmen living along the banks of the Rio Grande--still known then as the Río Bravo--felt themselves as separate from Mexico City as the people of New Spain had been from Madrid. So they adopted a new identity, calling themselves *tejanos*.

The border on the Sabine was replaced by one further southwest in 1836, when the state of Tejas seceded from Mexico and declared itself an independent, Anglo-dominated republic. A fiery debate ensued between Mexico City and Austin over the question of where Mexico ended and Texas began, with Texians and Tejanos arguing their new republic stretched all the way to the Río Bravo, while Mexicans insisted the Nueces River had always marked the boundary between old Tejas and the rest of Mexico. At the time, much of the area, including what would become eastern New Mexico and West Texas, was home to the Comanche, an unruly tribe of horsemen who displayed their hostility to Texian and Tejano colonizers alike by raiding settlements in and around a vast territory decidedly named the Comancheria.

    Farther west, Mexico continued Spain's effort to keep the Russian Empire from venturing any further south than the Russian colonial settlement at Fort Ross, in present-day Sonoma County. (Russia eventually abandoned its claims south of Alaska to the British and United States, with the two empires arguing over the territory north of Mexico's Alta California for decades afterward.) Meanwhile, the age of the Spanish missions in Alta California was coming to a close. Beginning in the 1830s, the Mexican government instituted a program of secularization, hoping to rein in the power of the Catholic Church. Presidios and missions were gradually eclipsed by the pueblos that had formed around them, places like Monterrey, San Diego, and El Pueblo de Nuestra Señora la Reina de los Ángeles, whose name would eventually be shortened. As in Texas, the area outside these burgeoning towns was still effectively controlled by native tribes--the Pomo north of San Francisco, the Chumash around San Luis Obispo, the Tvonga near Pasadena, and many others-- who had been enslaved and nearly Hispanicized under the regime of the Spanish missionaries; now they were forced to contend with increasing colonization from settlers who didn't consider themselves Mexicans either, but Californios. And, in what would become the southern parts of Arizona and New Mexico, the Mexican army waged a hundred years of war against various Apache tribes well into the twentieth century.

The border dispute between the Mexicans and the Anglos was settled, in a way, when the United States annexed the Republic of Texas in 1845 and declared war on Mexico only a few months later, looking to fulfill the empire's self-imposed destiny to extend its western border to the Pacific Ocean and beyond, or, as President Polk promised in his inaugural address, "to extend the dominions of peace over additional territories and increasing millions." The Treaty of Guadalupe Hidalgo, which ended the war in 1848, saw Mexico lose the northern half of its pre-1836 territory, and set the Rio Grande as the natural boundary between the state of Texas and Mexico; the Gadsden Purchase in 1854, which settled the southern borders of Arizona and New Mexico, saw Mexico give up even more land. Yet for all intents and purposes, the newly acquired Southwest was still greatly uncharted, with Apaches lurking up in the Chiricahua Mountains, Navajos sheltering in Canyon de Chelly, and Comanches dominating the Texas plains. Only after a series of onslaughts--against the Navajo in the 1860s, against the Comanche in the 1870s, and against the Apache in the 1880s--did the U.S. and Mexican governments feel secure enough to form a commission charged with defining the boundary between their two countries once and for all.

If the first half of the border's history was dominated by disputes over land, then the second half has centered on conflicts over people. The Mexican Revolution marked the beginning of United Statesians' long-held preoccupation with who or what might be traveling across their southern border. At the time, Pancho Villa and other banditos were the enemy border-crossers; in the 1930s, and then again in the 1950s, migrant workers were said to be streaming over the border and stealing jobs away from *actual Americans* (though the people of Mexico, along with the rest of Latin America, are actually Americans too). Since President Nixon declared a "War on Drugs" in 1971, it has been the Mexican drug smuggler whom we must keep out; the attacks on September, 2001, added terrorists to the growing number of foreign threats; and now, following the economic collapse of 2008, job-stealing Mexicans once again top the list of reasons to secure the border with Mexico.

      This story--the story of the border *and its people*--is the subject of the present anthology. As its title suggests, *Poets Facing the Wall* comes as a direct response to the latest attack on borderlands society: President Trump's proposed border wall. ("I would build a great wall," Trump said when he announced his bid for the White House in June 2015. "I will build a great, great wall on our southern border, and I'll have Mexico pay for that wall.") The purpose of the wall, according to him, would be to keep people living south of the border from crossing north and "bringing drugs [and] crime" (and "rapists"), but this, of course, is pure rhetoric--immigrants are no more dangerous than the rest of the general public, and statistically even less so. The wall's true *raison d'être* is as a sop to the nativists and xenophobes in the Republican base, who voted for Trump in 2016 hoping he would help preserve the United States as a Anglo-Christian domain and, so long as millions of Anglo-Christians are out of work or otherwise struggling to make ends meet, keep decent-paying jobs out of the hands of non-whites--which, for this rabble, includes Latinos of *any* color. And, as it did in China and in Britain, and as it continues to in Palestine and Northern Ireland, the wall, even the mere talk of building one, is meant as an affront to those living on the other side, and as a warning: *Keep out!... No vacancy... No soliciting... Trespassers will be shot!*

The wall itself would be a five-billion-dollar boondoggle. "Because a river that cuts between countries is not enough," Kristin Barendsen writes ironically in *Poets Facing the Wall*. Anyone who has traveled along the border, and gazed over its seemingly monolithic landscape, may echo Teri Garcia-Ruiz, who asks in her single-sentence poem, "Wide Open," "Where is the checkpoint/ For the breeze blowing over/ The river today?" "Clouds," notes Robbi Nester, "easily evade barbed wire." For her part, the poet and educator Xánath Caraza wonders, "What is a border?" before offering her own sense: "Created limits/ cultures forced/ to turn their back." Sandra Anfang uses every letter in the alphabet to describe the wall--"fence/ garrison/ hoosegow/ impediment/ jacket/ kennel"--none of her terms suggesting safety.

A great deal of the poems dwell on the human toll wrought by the United States's increasing militarization of its southern border. "The Wall is not Safety," Miranda Rocha insists, "it's a blow to the heart/ I must ask, why can't we just come together?/ Let's eat good food and make art." (Hear, hear!) Catherine Lee compares two kinds of being held: "Held in your parent's arms, with love/ secured by a same-blood bond against fear," on the one hand, and on the other, "Held against your will, by force of arms/ ripped from your parent's arms sobbing." The very first line of a blues song by Laurie Jurs puts it plainly: "There's bloodstains at the border."

Other poems speak to the cost that U.S. border policies have had on the once heralded American Dream-- the dream being that a free and diverse country could actually exist and succeed. In "Song for America XXV," Flores describes the United States as "a land where freedom rings/ From a fenced in lot/ Promoting a plastic posterity." "America," Richard Nester assures us, "has always existed/ better in the minds of its immigrants than anywhere else"; and in "Lament for Emma Lazarus," he writes frankly, "I miss/ America, or/ what I thought/ it was." Sharon Lundy contrasts the "bittersweet goodbye[s]" portrayed in "Tinseltown" to the family separations carried out by Border Patrol--"Children are ripped/ From their mother's arms/ To be put in cages/ Screaming"--while Rocha's "Liberty and the Pursuit of Happiness" ends with a sad realization: "They told us America is the land of the Free/ But The Wall clearly states, you must buy Liberty." Sunayna Pal sums it all up in "Myopia of belonging" by saying, "there are many lies that we learn/ but nothing beats patriotism."

    The rest of the poems in this anthology are mixture of wrath and grief, heartache and contempt--much of it aimed at President Trump and his cohort. C. R. Resetarits labels Trump's wall "a monument to furtive demagoguery," while Flores, in "Song for America XXVIII," renames the White House "the outhouse" and says of our national motto, "E pluribus unum united in one hate." "Look at my hands," cries Vanessa Caraveo, embodying a *bracera* speaking her mind to the anti-immigrant crowd; "Do you really think I crossed the border for this?" Roger Sippl wishes we could "Go back ... to what we *now* know was safe, even though it was scary enough./ The people were the people/ we knew, and trusted, or knew/ not to trust." ("But," he realizes a couple lines later, "they're the same/ as they always were.") Anfang, prefacing another poem with a quote from Mussolini, wants to "build a ten-foot wall around him [Trump]/ to procure his safety/ from the sweat of labor/ the bane of blackness and Latin fever/ shield him from the blood/ that feeds the onion field/ and greases the wheels of commerce." Jill Evans regrets how our "stubborn grudges/ cling to us like fumes," and "this speechless rage/ that floats upon us/ in such easy reach/ that it eclipses reason." But then again, Evans affirms, "it is our time": "Here, hold tight to the bravery of/ the word, the song, even the sob, as if it were a helping hand."

Evans' words, along with the others in this anthology, remind me of the real power that poetry wields. Poets can compel the oppressed to "rise like lions," or, as Auden put, and as these poets have done, "make a vineyard of the curse." Auden, in the same poem, eulogizing the recently deceased Yeats in 1939, infamously stated that "poetry makes nothing happen," and while I, as a boy coming up in an illiterate milieu, once thought the same, I don't for a moment believe it now (and judging by his polemical poems, neither did Auden--not really.) I'm much more inclined to side with Shelley, who, in his "Defence of Poetry," calls poets "the mirrors of the gigantic shadows which futurity casts upon the present; the words which express what they understand not; the trumpets which sing to battle, and feel not what they inspire; the influence which is moved not, but moves. Poets," he declares, "are the unacknowledged legislators of the world." This is true-- but if only it were *more* true.

After reading the beautiful verses published here, we are still left with a border and, possibly, a wall. What to do? What *can* we do? We can rally, we can march, we can call our senators and congresspeople, we can donate our time and money to worthy organizations, we can call for the demilitarization of the border, we can study the border, its history, and its people--we can and should do all of those things. But what we cannot do, what must not do, is turn our backs on the issues. We must exercise what Orwell called the "power of facing unpleasant facts," and the U.S.-designed humanitarian crisis at the border--plus Trump's promised wall--are unpleasant facts, very and truly.

Let this anthology stand as a message to the enemies of peace in the borderlands, on both sides: We stand united, *against you*. And let it serve as a rallying cry to our allied brothers and sisters: We offer you these soaring words--but, should words not be enough, we will fight off any injustice with "our gathering fists."

An Inheritance of Fear
By Jill Evans

Here,
hold the word, the song, even the sigh,
as if it were a helping hand. Here,
lean slowly towards its keening sound.

Quick, as the crash comes
rumbling home, consider
all the fallout
of our very best intentions.

Here, this is the first time,
an echo of once again,
when it is we who must
pick through the rubble.
This time it is our time, our walls,
our towering immunity
brought down onto this common
crumbled surface of our disbelief.

Here in a mushroom cloud of sorrow,
through the amber dust of lunacy,
here while suspicions whirl like asbestos
into our pores with a cyclone's pull,
pay cautious homage here

to the tall, aspiring towers
that just disappeared,
raining untamed symbols
in bitter air.

Hush. Stay silent here
with our new emerging pain.
Keep step, keep pace, keep peace
with our unfolding grief.
Warn the flags
that unfurl nameless fists
into the lowered eyelid of the sun.

Now here, excavate, dig deep
for even older shrouds at this disaster's edge.
Turn the searchlight on this land
seasoned by our prejudice,
where stubborn grudges
cling to us like fumes,
invisible as gravity.

And slow
this speechless rage
that floats upon us
in such easy reach
that it eclipses reason
in a creeping dread.

For this time, it is

here. Our gathering fists.
Our feral fear. For above all, we
must be most careful
with what unites us now.

Here, hold tight to the bravery of
the word, the song, even the sob,
as if it were a helping hand…

As We Forgive Those
By Roger Sippl

The angel is still on top of the tree
but the Pope is trying to change the lyric
of the Our Father. What we want

is no change. Go back, even,
to what we *now* know was safe,
even though it was scary enough.

The people were the people
we knew, and trusted, or knew
not to trust. So, we think

we don't know these new people
now, but they're the same
as they always were.

The prayer world is in turmoil,
but haven't there always
been multiple translations

of everything we believe?

Ave Blanca
Seres Jaime Magaña

Veo un ave atada a la espalda de la bestia
Viene de mares de fruta
Tierra de volcanes
Ave blanca, ave viajera
A donde vas la tierra sangra
Le entregas tus alas al silencio
Eres un sol escondido en el arbusto, ardiendo
Tus pies espinados por el nopal
Y en ruta a la nada

No importa un paraíso de calles limpias
No importa cuantos sabores y texturas se puedan envolver en plástico
No importa que tan inmediato llega el placer, igual de rápido se va

Veo un ave atada a la espalda de la bestia
Llena de esperanza
Una aventura encarcelada en su alma

Y no importa la altura de nuestro reino
Construido de ceniza y hueso
Lo único que importa
Es ver esa ave volar

Blue Again
By C. R. Resetarits

This bridge in moonlight spans mythic worlds,
cottonwoods are avenging furies
overwrought by wind, mesquites
are hydras, sage lost souls. This bridge
is built of fragments, slights, tricks of law,
amassed in alchemical tracts, in columns
of seeping rust and beam and prayer.
Empty now but for water echoes,
but for fret lines across the moon's
blueprint, for tree lined banks stirring.

We see blossoms of loss falling through
branches, as cuts, as galls, as bits of sky.
A flashpoint, signal, a confusing thing.
It stops us in our tracks, stops us in our
dismissing that other bridge upstream
a monument to furtive demagoguery
which is all the blue this moment needs
as our injuries skim steep mud banks
slick as steel toward salves too swift
and we tremble and cry but begin again.

BLUES FOR JOSE ANTONIO ELENA RODRIGUEZ
(Traditional 12 Bar Blues Song)
by Laurie Jurs

There's bloodstains at the border, on Calle Internacional
There's bloodstains at the border, on Calle Internacional
Where they shot Jose Antonio, thirty feet beneath The Wall

It was a late October night, they said he threw some rocks
It was a late October night, they said he threw some rocks
They dropped him on the pavement, with ten gunshots

It's forty feet straight up to the top of The Wall
It's forty feet straight up to the top of The Wall
Any rock that cleared it would be no threat at all

Where is the justice? Where is the truth?
Where is the justice? Where is the truth?
If there's nothing to hide, then show us the proof

A cold-eyed camera sits high above the site
A cold-eyed camera sits high above the site
We want to know what it saw that night

Three years later, we can hear his mother's cry
Three years later, we can hear his mother's cry
She'll never understand why her boy had to die

Agent Lonnie Swartz, tell us what you saw
Agent Lonnie Swartz, tell us what you saw
Then tell it to the judge in a court of law

You've been charged with murder in the second degree
You've been charged with murder in the second degree
    You might go to prison and you might go free

There's bloodstains at the border, on Calle Internacional
There's bloodstains at the border, on Calle Internacional
Where they shot Jose Antonio, thirty feet beneath The Wall

Construction of First Border Wall Segment to Begin in a South Texas Wildlife Refuge
By Kristin Barendsen

In this place where flyways converge,
    where wings rest from long migrations to the four directions,
In this zone where ecologies overlap,
      where tropics merge with wetlands, desert, coast, and plains,
On this land where mythical creatures are still embodied
    and ocelots hunt nine-banded armadillos
    and jaguarundis yowl across the river to find their mates
—

Here, the bulldozers are scheduled to break ground first.
Here, the concrete mixers are slated to dump their contents first
    to build a levee higher
        than some birds can fly, higher
        than six of my bodies standing feet on shoulders.

Because the ocelots don't have papers
    and the jaguarundis are coming for your job
        and willing to work for food.
Because the *coyotes* traffic in humans as well as rabbits.

    Because a river that cuts between countries
        is not enough—
    we must have a knife blade severing the earth,
        dividing wing from sky,
        peeling fur from skin.

Because extinction is what we strive toward these days:
Extinction of those endangered cats,
    of the migratory birds
        flying in from Brazil and Colombia,
    of the migratory families
        smuggled in from Mexico and Ecuador.
Extinction of immigration,
    of human decency,
        and eventually of humanity.

Because a concrete wall is a way to separate javelina from
javelina | heron from nest | *madre*
    from *niño* | us from them | white fur from brown wing
And a concrete wall will erase the footprints the tracks |
silence the birdsong, yowls, cries |
    collect bones at its base. Because a concrete wall higher
than six of my bodies standing feet on shoulders
    will be a deathtrap in hurricane country
        keeping tongues from meeting river when it's dry
        blocking flight away from river when it floods.

I want to make my body into a bridge over that wall
    let the cat claws walk my back
    guide a flock of land birds toward their habitat.

I want to make my spine a stairway so deported Dreamers
can climb back,
    slide down my arms on the other side
I'll be the corridor that wildlife need to survive,
    the trail, the path, the overpass.

Feet to hands, my curve will span longer than a skyway,
    stretch wider than a two-lane road

So I can take the weight of whole families without trembling,
    hide children in my pockets when ICE comes looking.
And at night when my arms rise, my body will become a ladder of stars
    leading to a boundless place.

I'll be that girded arc until
Spanish moss drips from my elbows,
    yellowthroats roost on my shoulders
        indigo snakes bracelet my ankles and
    tropical butterflies explore the blooms of my ears my lips.

I'll be the refuge
    where travelers have a place to rest
    and hook-billed kites can make their nest
        with strands of my graying hair.

THE DIFFERENCE BETWEEN HELD AND HELD
by Catherine Lee

Held in your parent's arms, with love
secured by a same-blood bond against fear,
a long list of unknown terrors
enumerated, caused by, encountered
throughout asylum journey
in the company of family
you would be held close.

then

Held against your will, by force of arms
ripped from parent's arms sobbing,
screaming loss, a child in pain
enclosed in chain link cage
in warehouse, freezing cold *hielera*
without defense against their fear
of 'others' like you,
so many of them acting out
their terror upon
your devalued alien flesh,
their compassion comatose.

We have to wonder why
they call their zero tolerance law approved,
mandated, justified by their
Bible's isolated verse.
We have to wonder how
they calculate that wailing cries of toddlers
mask play acting by political design.
They hear orchestral choir

missing its conductor
for unpleasant shows.

Indeed, missing is a veritable leader
someone who could guide
these mutually shared encounters
to harmony, satisfactory concession.

We have to wonder,
were they ever held by someone who
could show them where to find a soul?
teach benefaction?
or

Were they merely held, caught by someone
going through the motions,
sparse partitioner of love
making extravagantly tough displays
of fashionable bloodline loyalty,
an ever shrinking ration?

We have to choose
caregiver-held opposed to captor-held relations
in our barb-wired world of different bordered nations.

My Exit
By Richard Nester

for Amiri Baraka
The word existential has been kicked around
so much lately that it hardly exists. I learned it
in high school, reading off the syllabus—
Sartre and Camus, No Exit and The Plague—
when the word meant something, at least to me.
An idea made real by acts is what it meant to me,
not doctrine or tradition or genetics—our prefab
guideposts. I'd had enough of those already,
clapboard sermons with their stained-glass
traditions and in my DNA, the boarded-shut
postures of relations over family dinners,
my family, who weren't immigrants any longer.
We'd been here too long, long enough to forget
when we first learned English and began to move
among our fellow citizens as though we were natives.

I learned about this reality teaching ESL
to California kids from Asia and Peru and Slovokia,
who stamped my passport. America has always existed
better in the minds of its immigrants than anywhere else,
in the blue suits of the Irish Iron Brigade at Gettysburg

and in the black and tan bodies of Negroes at The Crater
in Petersburg on their way to liberating Richmond.

Donald Trump has re-branded Amerika.
Have you tried to read his signature? If you didn't
know who it was doing the signing, you'd never
figure it out. It's a wall. At least, John Hancock,
peacock though he may have been, wrote
a hand could be read.

In nightmares I dream that I'm a Democrat congressman
forced to vote for THE WALL (tweet, tweet) in order to get
DACA.
Then I realize I'm awake. Big D, dilemma! Blake told us,
an idea can be a wall too, once you erase its human
components.

Existential was a part of something I could call myself,
though not in public (just me speaking to me like
an understanding friend), trusting its too cool but ever
faithful feel—more real somehow than being a Baptist.
Now it seems forever joined to the word— threat.

I'll leave the South for the last time
when my father dies—his "existential" death,
my exit.

The Greatest, Most Beautiful Soliloquy EVER!
By Rick Blum

To tweet, or not to tweet: that is the question
Whether 'tis nobler in my mind to suffer
The crooked slings and arrows of failing flacks
Or take up thumbs against a sea of inquest
To die, to sleep: perchance to dream of revenge:
Ay, there's the rub, for what stiff dreams may reveal
When we've been deleted from this mortal coil
Must give us pause: there's no respect for losers
For who would bear the whips and scorns of Maddow
The oppressor's wrongs, insults of proud McCain
I grunt and sweat in this voracious life, while
Billions and billions dread doom after death
Thus conscience 'tis only for huge cowards
Weak to missives of great pith and moment
With this regard my bad currents rage bigly
To win in the name of bold action: I TWEET!

Ten Commandments Updated
By Rick Blum

> *- And God gazed upon his earthly creation and decided his laws for moral behavior, passed down to Moses three millennia ago, desperately needed updating. So He did.*

I

Thou shalt have no other gods before me, no matter how many stars are on the epaulets of their uniforms, or zeros follow their estimated net worth in *Forbes* magazine.

II

Thou shalt not make unto thee any graven image by gilding thy penthouse floors, walls, sofas, loveseats, chandeliers, and bathroom fixtures, or splashing thy name on hotel facades, airplane fuselages, and steaks.

III

Thou shalt not take the name of the Lord thy God in vain, nor refer to others as Liddle, Crooked, Crazy, Psycho, Flakey, Rocket Man, Sleepy Eyes, or Pocahontas. Lyin' Ted is OK.

IV

Remember the Sabbath day; to keep it holy, no golfing or Fox News watching is permitted ... until after thou hast read the Presidential Daily Brief cover-to-cover (no skimming allowed).

V

Honor thy father and thy mother, as well as every contract thou hast signed no matter how badly doing so will crater thy bottom line.

VI

Thou shalt not kill a bill to ban assault weapons, or expand healthcare access, or give "Dreamers" a path to citizenship.

VII

Thou shalt not commit adultery, even with a porn star or Playmate who reminds you of your daughter – *especially* not with a porn star or Playmate who reminds you of your daughter.

VIII

Thou shalt not steal elections by gerrymandering congressional districts to make voting an exercise in futility.

IX

Thou shalt not bear false witness before Robert Mueller.

X

Thou shalt not covet a second term unless thou art prepared to be humiliated bigly, which I guarantee will happen if thou breaketh any of the preceding Commandments.

Guardian of the Mountains
By Michael Garrigan

Checkpoint #1
We were where desert meets pine to cut chaparral and clear downed trees.
Santa Ana winds ripped our tents, breathing ice across breakfast
faces blistered by cold sand, buried in a grit cloth.

Checkpoint #2
A borderland desert landscape bounds a quebrada of cottonwoods -
thin grass and a sliver of a stream - in the Hauser Wilderness.
Shirts pants bags baby formula wind clustered around trees, caught in sage.
Ornaments of Migration.

We drink, Dave's long white hair sticks to his spine. He nods at the piles.
I only drink coffee and beer. I carry water for them. I say in Spanish:
Yo soy el guardián de las montañas.
La gente viene aquí para estar más cerca de Dios.
Tengo comida y agua que compartiré contigo.
If it wasn't for Mexicans we wouldn't know what a strawberry is.

Checkpoint #3
On day six we stop for lunch along a switchback
after cutting trail all morning and watch
border patrol scurry like recluse spiders

along highways cutting Laguna Mountains.
Your shoulders covered by a ratty blanket stuck with briars, matted with dirt
you cradle your plastic bottle so the creek water won't spill out of the hole.
Your jeans heavy wet with sweat frozen at night thawed each morning.
We give you water and trail mix and beef jerky.
Did you make it? Or are you bloated gray green?
Are vultures circling overhead, hide beatles eating
the hard dried tissue? Did you find your father?
You keep walking north.
We have trail to cut.

I Am Chicano
By Sammy Ybarra

Yo soy Chicano ..I am Chicano, y es todo
Its me ... soy yo
This land is my Land . Aqui esta tierra
..es mia .. de nacimiento
My foundation ..the beginning of it all
.. my blood ... it runs deep
From way back .. beyond the time
of the norm of things, of awareness and of sleep
When Aztecs . when Incas . when the Yaqui
..tambien .all of Life to behold
A beautiful world . untouched by other men
as it has been written ...as it has been told
Generations have rooted, lived and walked this wonder ..
of Coastline, Desert, Mountains .. and More
The window of life, here .. ever changing
..another chapter, beyond the door
By the time my father's father ..completed his long
journey, his walk of life
A border line drawn ..with a pulse given
so they listened .. to this talk of strife
Of a treaty ..of language .and of culture
homeowners keeping their Land
But, Like so many others .. they found ..'mentiras'
.. ..'keeping nothing' ..its a Demand
"All that are here come truthful and clear...
and give all your possessions and goods"
This came to include .. entire families who
found themselves separated and misunderstood
With history .. only mistreatment and lies
evolved a revolutionary seed

Its the nature of the beast ..my branch on
this tree ..'leaves' out all that i need
My early years ..those all around
daily living .. it mirrors to me
Each day, a dose of happiness and love
..how wonderful ..my life as it be
Yo soy Chicano .. I am Chicano ...
its meaning, not to know . nor what it seems
Its living within my soul every day
and every Day, is what it means
So i ride this life journey .. a slide show
of stories and tales
made of family and heros, friendships
cartoons .. coloring at school and lunch pales
From Logan Heights to Paradise Hills .. our
President in Dallas ..and grown men would cry
I watched it all unfold on TV .. .a little boy
salutes ... his dad goes by
Once a year my father .. took us all
..to Tijuana

To watch a parade, i do remember
It was Independence Day in Mexico
the parade .. the 16th of September
And on the Fourth of July .. our celebration
to the beach .. with chips, hot dogs and sodas
This yearly event passed on thru fireworks
to picnics .. and dances ..and Bodas
Yo soy Chicano .. I am Chicano
Ballete Foklorico .. high ranking Boy Scout
After school bus ride ..pop warner practice
Otay Lakes with my Dad, catching Trout
Back home en mi casa .. a world of intrig .. creative

minds .. family and love
Every nite, my 'Mother', home from work
my Mom ..our Lite, our Peaceful Dove
By now i know .. the History of this Land
of my Family .. and all of its past
Con Mariachi y Corridos .. Rock & Roll
and Soul music . how long would all of it last
We spoke english in our schools .. we
heard Spanish at my Nana's .. Que no?
As an Altar Boy .. the Catholic mass .. a part
of it all, but the Latin .. had to go!
So what was I, a little Mexican boy
I pledge alligence to the flag .. high above
Singing Yankee Doodle Dandy with a
song and a dance .. 'Mananitas' to my
mom, with Love
Our homes, never without our Heritage
or Culture ..a compromising page
I was singing .. I was acting ..every day
life ..for me? a wide open, musical stage
Like a shot out of the dark .. awakening our
minds ..into our Souls and into our Home
The heartbeat of Cesar Chavez, nuestra Causa
La Huelga! .. and a Life of its Own
One by one .. my brothers ..my mother ..and
my father ..ventured down that path
The boycotts ..Delano ..Campesinos in the fields
Not just a story, but 'Our' Grapes of Wrath
Yo Soy Chicano .. I Am Chicano
I am all of the things .. none of the same
You, who put titles ..or say what it should be
Its our life .. our living, that's given Its name
As the Days, turning Weeks, into Months

through the Years, a Life Long, so it seems
The never ending .. page after page of growing
older ..my Heritage, my flag and my Dreams
Several Great stories in the mind of one Lifetime
an overwhelming sense of 'being' ..by far
Engulfed with the Spirit of Chicano studies
the pioneers..what they lived ... who they are

Juan deDios Gonzalez my grandfather, organized
to fight school segregation .. and won!
With my grandmother and their fourteen children
..my Family's mark, on Greatness to come
Richard Ybarra .. my Mother's son, my brother ...
his way of doing .is what we would do ..
He put the C H in character .. R Y in everything ..
and with class, sang "The Basin Street Blues"..
I'd have it no other way .. what the voices would say
all the battles ..all the issues at hand
I was as American and Free as the gringo next door
and my Mexico .. .this Is my Land
My family and friends, my city, my state ..
the southwest .. and across the blue sea
Over the years ..would come to know and experience
my magical journey ..'Music and Me'
I never lost site nor stopped feeling the pain
of what my Raza endured .. and it's all
Here i stayed living .. keeping close to my heart ..
winter, spring, summer and fall
Yo Soy, I Am, Chicano .. at times Mexico
the USA .. seemed to not want us around
Down south, just pochos to them, up here
cuz of skin color, 'beautiful brown'
Not much of this mattered to the Love of my Life

from Rich Coast .. Aztec Princess .. Latin Queen
With Love in her heart .. this serpent of Mexico
was her choice .. fulfilling a dream
As the sun would set, all the moments we met
couldnt prepare us or meet the demand
Tho we answered the call ..we stand strong and tall
Put our Love in God's holy hands
Injustice and greed .. a world of hate plants a seed
..second class my people are treated
So we marched and we voted .. some drank .. others
loaded ..elected our own to be seated
I say then ..catch yourself before getting
caught up in the retoric of "what means who"
Your definitions. criteria of being ..no need for
proof here ..to Me or to You
Telling someone what Chicano is ..or isnt, estas
palabras ..separadas, just turn in the mud
To be brothers, me to you ..you to me, as the eagle flies
our spirit ..nuestra sangre, Chicano blood!
Our Lives are long .. our legacy is 'Longer'
we live life .. we give life ..we continue, 'Stronger'
Like the Phoenix Bird ...about to perish in the 'Flame'
we emerge ..we endure .. from this shadow of 'Pain'
As warmth for our bodies and light for the world
.. cleansing the soul and sharpen our mind
With the sun in our hearts .. and sites to behold
a Golden star, Chicano Nation will find
A star ..thats what we reach for ... throughout

time spent .. on journey's door
It should matter not .. what hat is worn
but our heart's love that matters more
Back to reality ..back to today ..we still

hear voices calling "close the Fronteras"
How do you close the air flow that breathes
life to the Living en esta Tierra
Its as natural as the rivers that flows to the sea
..or the summer wind that gives in to the Fall
The evening stars that lite up the nite
or the Sun that shines over it all
Then, to hear from my own not living as shown?
There's no need, somos hermanos .. asi es
We have sacrificed .. survived ..we are rich
and we are poor .. and, we have been blessed
Our struggle is long ..we still fight for our land
nuestra tierra .. todos los dias
With each breath i take, i live and i die
Yo soy Chicano .. la sangre mia
I am Chicano .. Chicano is what it is
It's what i am .. I..It is me
By sacred right of my family .. my blood
here, in Mexico ... in Califas .. Aqui
And the red white and blue .. that, of many
i knew .. died for the rights i attain
An inherited domain and a flag that came
to be my life ..thru the sun and the rain
Yaqui blood, the Spirit of Zacatecas, footprints
of Christianity and Wisdom, 'freedom of mind'
Explored ..this vast golden land, with its Majesty,
with its History .. with its Me .. and it finds
I am the Serpent of Mexico, from upon a rock,
from the wind of the plains and cactus done
I am crashing waves that have merged from the
sea.. and the Brown eyed children of the Sun
Nothing and no one on the face of the Earth
can take my spirit or the face of my name

You soy Chicano ..I am Chicano
as the eagle soars ..i am one in the same
With each breath i take ..i live and i die
Yo soy .. I Am, Chicano .. Am I
. . . Esta, es mi Sangre! . . .

Liberty and the Pursuit of Happiness
By Miranda Rocha

They told us America is the land of the Free
Where you may seek happiness and Liberty,
But everywhere I go I have to be afraid
That people will turn on me once they hear my last name

I wish we could all live together
Instead of being condemned
I once had a woman hear me speak Spanish
She looked at me in surprise and asked,
"Oh my God, you're one of them?"

When I was a child we were taught in school
That America is the land of the Free
But as I've grown there's a constant battle within me
I don't understand what people want us to be
When they separated us from our families
With The Wall in between

I heard a heartbroken cry from Lady Liberty
Who had welcomed all with a smile,
She'd said, "Why don't you stay a while?"
I watched the tears fall from her eyes
I heard her whispers in the winds say, "Why"
We've been crying for our families
We've been torn apart

The Wall is not Safety, it's a blow to the heart
I must ask, why can't we just come together?
Let's eat good food and make art
Let us not separate ourselves with this Wall

If we put our heads together we could have it all
Lady Liberty lit the way with her torch
But The Wall has done nothing but leave our hearts scorched

They told us America is the land of the Free
But The Wall clearly states, you must buy Liberty.

'You Make the Call'
by Sammy Ybarra

My brothers, my sisters, my fellow human beings
we all live here together, every one of us has dreams
Whether generations past or new comers just beginning
we want to feel excitement, that of life and that of living
What better way to feel, in your heart of heart each day
that you are welcomed, you belong and you are here to stay
By sacred rights your family from past or recent years
gives you the feeling, admission paid in peace and not in fear
History shows that 'Liberty' welcomed all who've come to live
with open arms many to one, to be productive and to give
To take upon themselves , to follow rules and to defend
collectively red white and blue, a fellow neighbor and a friend
Diversity, the mighty key making this nation oh so great
has been a source of strength the inner visions of our fate
Now comes along this negative, to divide of yours and mine
a Wall to stop the very people, been here thru all of time
How dare this group, powers to be, the elected few of many
try to pretend to be your friend with bad intentions plenty
Have they forgotten, with only truth that History does not lie
Mexican blood of which 'this was' has defended and has died
Said today that from the south, only bad men hand in hand
criminals that rape and kill bringing drugs into this land
Yet facts be told that isn't so, among the millions that have come

are doctors, lawyers, teachers, a labor force that's number one
The manifest of destiny by which this nation to be created
a forgotten key that willingly speaks of taken and sedated
The border to the north majestic mountains, rivers, trees
left alone over the years to live its beauty, open and free
But this mighty nation under God, with it's justice for all
will have to stand and make demand before we take a fall

Need to hold these truths, 'created equal', all one in the same
don't need a wall to divide the land, we know each other's name
Oh Mexico, my Mexico you have suffered through the years
half of you was taken away, the other half left with tears
We cant deface this land and tear a hole across its heart
dividing those of our own blood and tearing us apart
We need to find a way to keep our neighbors as our friends
to live together side by side, help to heal and to mend
The many years our father's father's toiled and have given
their lives of labor and sacrifice for us, a better livin
What contribution to history how dare we try and seed
a new way of living by leaving out all those in need
There is but one God looking down on us, He see's it all
with no mistake and do what's right, You make the Call

Myopia of belonging
By Sunayna Pal

Falling and fouling
as we grow up
Intentionally and Un
there are many lies that we learn
but nothing beats patriotism.
Just because,
we are born in a particular street
or town or district or state
or country or continent or planet
doesn't make it better
or worth fighting for.
Inexisting differences
separate you
blind you
to the good in everyone.
See with your heart's eyes
the mistakes you make
and the lives you take
in the name of God
when you trouble
his children.

Northward Bound
By Ana Maria Fores Tamayo

Darkness with light: it approaches surreptitiously
creeping red across the skies littered white and blue and gray.
Its beauty threatened by unruly nightfall, darkness making black its king.
There dreamed a starless sky, littered with catastrophic clouds
as wolves howl at the reverie of moon.
Blue sunsets spill their purpled vanity
against the round globe smearing shadow twilight
to its mountain greens...
But the darkness of destruction past
does not seem to settle on the tired smiles of weathered women
walking to a beaconed light,
searching for a peace of heaven,
waiting for salvation in the prayers offered by their seasoned hopes,
holding out a candle to guide their threatened path.

Hacia El Norte
by Ana Maria Fores Tamayo

Oscuridad con luz: se acerca silencioso
un rojo rastrando el cielo cubierto de blanco, azul y gris.
Su belleza amenaza un anochecer rebelde; su oscuridad la
negrura hace rey.
Se sueña un cielo sin estrellas, plagado de nubes
catastróficas
como lobos que aúllan la quimera de una luna llena.
Las puestas de sol azules derraman su vanidad violeta
contra el claro globo untando su sombra crepuscular
a sus frondosas montañas verdes ...
Pero la oscuridad de la pasada destrucción
no se fija en las cansadas risas de mujeres desgastadas
caminando hacia la luz del norte,
buscando una paz del cielo,
esperando salvación en oraciones ofrecidas por viejas
esperanzas,
sosteniendo una vela para guiar ese camino desafiado aun.

Oh, Say Can You See
By Wendy Baron

I hear America crashing

As shrieking sirens blast

Our creeds no longer mingled

In the dream that was meant to last

Collective amnesia hovers

Over our immigrant past

Wedges driven growing

Into the dream that was meant to last

The Great Society shrunken

And split between rich or not

No deal- old nor new deal

For those with less to their lot

The pot is near to boiling

Confrontation near to starts

And what then must we do

For the whole to be more than its parts?

On Day 1, We Will Begin Working
By Natalie D-Napoleon

"The Wall is the Wall
a wall, a real
wall."

build a wall a great wall
big beautiful doors
openings in that wall
a wall

borders barriers the wall

the
southern border, lots of sun, lots of heat the wall
a solar wall
a big, fat beautiful door the wall
a wall

walls
the wall

a great wall,
a crummy wall a wall
beautiful door
a wall? a fence? a wall?

the Great Wall
the wall. The Wall's,
a wall

a wall
any wall
"On the fence - It's a wall.
build a fence

climb over"
the wall will be
'beautiful.'

(Erasure created from source text: Nixon, Ron, and Linda Qiu. "Trump's Evolving Words on the Wall." The New York Times, 18 Jan. 2018. Accessed 20 March, 2018, https://www.nytimes.com/2018/01/18/us/politics/trump-border-wall-immigration.html)

FRONTEXTO #98
1. He intentado borrar líneas
que marcan territorios
2. Solo el viento cuatropatas
no reconoce límites

FRONTEXTO #105
Soy vaca
en mi sueño
y vuelo sobre
muros
construidos
para evitar
que me
e
n
a
m
o
r
e
Tengo pie humano
y pezuña que te atraviesa
cuando me
despiertas

Soy vaca en mi sueño y vuelo sobre muros

Construidos para evitar que me enamore
Tengo pie humano y pezuña que te atraviesa cuando me despiertas

FRONTEXTO #139
¿Estas serán personas?
¿Estos son animales?

FRONTEXTO #152

Virgen de los inmigrantes crucificada
Virgen de todos los animales del desierto crucificada
Virgen de los niños separados de sus padres crucificada
Virgen de la frontera crucificada
Virgen de los coyotes arrepentidos crucificada
Virgen de los que esperan crucificada
Virgen de los que no regresan crucificada
Virgen de los que sobreviven matanzas crucificada
Virgen del Río Grande crucificada
Virgen de los apuñalados por la esperanza crucificada
Virgen de los que ya no tienen miedo crucificada
Virgen nuestra, virgen de nadie ruega por nosotros

virgen de los inmigrantes — crucificada
virgen de todos los animales — crucificada
del desierto
virgen de los niños separados — crucificada
de sus padres
virgen de — cru-
la frontera — ci-
— fi-
— ca-
— da
virgen de — crucificada
los coyotes — crucificada
arrepentidos
virgen de los
que esperan
virgen de los — crucificada
que no regresan
virgen de los — crucificada
que sobreviven
las matanzas
virgen del — crucificada
Río Grande
virgen de — crucificada
los que
apuñalan la esperanza
virgen de los que ya no tienen miedo
— crucificada

Border Crossings
by Natalie D-Napoleon

checkpoints

share a native tongue
hot spots for
control, and

crossings

weathered signs and asphalt

connecting

movements,

absurd

once

ambitious empires

destined to pursue
discomfort

my memories the lines of the
map

(Erasure created from source text: Sturgis, Sam. "Photographing Europe's Abandoned Border Crossings." City Lab.com, Nov 13, 2014, https://www.citylab.com/transportation/2014/11/photographing-the-eus-abandoned-border-crossings/382708/)

A Fluid Border
by Natalie D-Napoleon

the river the border between

a thorn

and home

Like A Highway

family used to cross
back
like a highway to get to
history
nervous

vulnerable in the Cold

this tiny patch of land

found out

and

held firm and swore she wouldn't leave

they

had to carry

the woman away

caution

tape

a crime scene

Don't look back. You are

forbidden

encased in cement
that river is gonna do what Mother taught it to

(Erasure poem created from source text: NPR Staff. "50 Years Ago, A Fluid Border Made The U.S. 1 Square Mile Smaller," NPR.org, 25 Sept. 2014. Accessed 27 Sept. 2014, http://www.npr.org/2014/09/25/350885341/50-years-ago-a-fluid-border-made-the-u-s-1-square-mile-smaller.)

Wide Open
By Teri Garcia-Ruiz

Where is the checkpoint
For the breeze blowing over
The river today?

                                  The Fool's Game
                                  By Teri Garcia-Ruiz

                                        Only a fool would
                             Flash his badge to stop the day
                               break when its' time comes

Blurred Vision
By Teri Garcia-Ruiz

You see it clearly;
You building it; them paying.
Your vision is wrong

denizen Z. two
by Steven Alvarez

                                                  yeah lost a lot of denizens | like |
                                                                lies but |
                                        purple | home | denizen Z.
              honeybun | you got all yr funny faces | questions |
                                                                      yeah . . .
                                                                    champ |
                                                             yeah you'll . . .
                                                good audio | add edge |
                                          the other corner but |
                                                yeah | highest |
                                          hotel | up like | oh |

huh | get somebody going on
| but |
| h.o..n.g n.h.u…n..g gas
rest the top |
doc | doc | okay
but yeah |
you |
in |
always | you | ok |
thank you
cocktail Polis A | canceling
it is the worst | action
you have
ever gone against | ones
that cannot
defend | selves |

this measure is cruel & heartless
worst than any machine | you cancel |
future | ninehundredthousand children | &young
people |
you are so mistaken
the future of any |
polis is the minorities which will be |
majorities in a few years you cannot |
stop | change the progress | future
of that great polis | you hope |

never be in this terrible |
situation

Blood, Sweat and Tears
By Vanessa Caraveo

Look at my hands
Do you really think I crossed the border for this?
To spend my days in arduous treacherous field work
Withstanding the scorching summer heat
Or unforgiving winter climate
Worst of all
For persons who think "we are stealing their jobs"
Malagradecidos!
Here is my heavy basket and sombrero
Take it
By all means pick up your own fruit and vegetables
That you gulp down every day with your loved ones at meals
Mis paisanos and I would like to see how long you can withstand this type of work.
Who would risk their own lives in vain?
Through the most unforgiving circumstances and terrain
If not for a better life and better future for themselves and their family?
If there is something I have in my heart it's to never coward down
And with courage to find a way for better days
I will always carry that value en mi corazon.
A wall is not the solution
It just creates an even bigger problem to much social injusticies that already exist
How can literally dividing us all even more do any good?
If what we need more of in today's world is unity.
I will continue doing my work with blood, sweat and tears

I am not embarrassed but honored to know I earn my
money through true hard labor
I will continue to dream and hope for better days
And to see the glorious day no river, nor border
Nor wall
Divides us
But the day we no longer judge a human being
On where they were born or where they come from
But for their essence and who they are
That day is the day we will finally be unidos.

Conflict
By Vanessa Caraveo

Being born in the US
Of Mexican descent
Seeing the news on tv
Depressing
That is what it all is.
I see the images of mi raza
Their struggle
Only to obtain a better life and future
I may not have been born on the other side
But I do have compassion.
I also hear the opinions of those in my country
Who share the same nationality as me
Americans
Feeling they are being stolen from
That there are rules to be followed.
I know many of us born in the US
And more so who live near the border
Also feel this internal conflict
Your people versus the country that gave you everything.
Expressing your opinion or perspective is the hardest thing
of all
It doesn't matter which side you take
You are going to be attacked by one side regardless
Be it by your race or your countrymen.
You will be marked as a traitor either way.
A wall?
If there are enough walls that already exists
Internally with so many as it is
No need to build another
Segregate us even more?

You have got to be kidding me.
We need to break these walls
Not build them
So we can have internal peace for everyone
No one should have to choose between the land they love
and their own people
No one.

Survival
By Vanessa Caraveo

No wall can ever stop a person who yearns for a better life
Someone who in many cases,
Knows if they stay in their country
They may not live to see another day literally.
No wall will prevent a loving parent who wants to provide a better future
To their offspring.
Being paid more than triple of what you're paid for to provide for your family
Compared to pennies on the dollar for your day-to-day hard labor
Is more than enough motivation to take the plight to a better place.
Yes you will face hostility
You will face discrimination
You will face many who don't understand you truly have no option
Than to move and leave everything behind
To truly survive.
And the human nature – it is our instinct to survive
So easy to judge until you and your loved ones
Are the ones needing to survive.
To you survivor,
Ignore the nay-sayers
No one risks their life
And many times their freedom
For an invaluable reason
You are not after the "American Dream"
You are after quite simply just general well-being
Is that too much to ask or understand?

Keep going
You've made it this far
Survive.

Hollywood
By Sharon Lundy

Tinseltown
Has a way of
Making us see the world
As we would like it
With perfectly scripted transitions
And a happy ending
But mothers
Do not always stand
Waving a bittersweet goodbye
To their child
Now grown
Eager to commence
Their own life
Sometimes
Children are ripped
From their mother's arms
To be put in cages
Screaming
As she pleads
And we sit
And watch
As if
It is simply
A movie

Musings
by Sheena Pillai Singh

He asked me
Why I love my GOD...
Dear, just let me say
life was been tough
all dark and grey
till HE came my way...

HE taught me
liberate,
not fall ,but rise
in LOVE...
be on my toes;
not to let it take
my good will for granted...

In you my GOD,
I lost the thin line
of Sin and Conscience
Sorrow and Pain,
Love and Worship..

I lost the days spent
seeking joy,
awaiting your call
those long nights
full of tears;
when your calls end .

Today as I recall
I lost the heavy burdens,
which I carried in my mind
all through the years…
I lost my GOD for ever

but to someone better...

Still I wish you Joy
Happiness and Peace
Now that you've found
Your Soul, Spirit and Light.

Song for America XXIII (the nation's anthem)
By Fernando Esteban Flores

If I stand
Or if I kneel
What does that reveal
Of the Nation's state—
The flag flies half staff
For our endangered species
No disrespect
For country
No malice toward
Those who gave their lives
In her defense
No hatred for those
Who sacrificed
What they had
That the machinery of democracy
Could go on
If I stand
Or if I kneel
The heart protests
The subtle lies
The political palaver
Of those who govern
For their gain
& stand before the flag
With two faced hands over shady hearts
The heart rebels against
The systemic wrongs
Poured out upon
The poor & powerless
The heart resists

The pointed blade of prejudice
The heavy hammer of oppression
The cold sickle of aggression
Unleashed by those sworn to
Keep the peace
The heart rejects
The cruel attempts
To suffocate
The voice of the oppressed

If I stand
Or if I kneel
The heart will not fail
Cower or bow
Before the walls of tyranny
Petty despots build
Wielding their weapons
Of cowardice hate fear
Sanctified & wrapped
In orchestrated stars & stripes
Dangling their false brands
With jingoistic jingles
Meant to numb the brain
Dull the heart
Pero el corazón no traicionará
Su propia verdad sagrada
But the heart will not betray
Its own sacred truth
Aunque por mil años
En cadenas espere
Thó it wait in chains
A thousand years

Song for America XXV
By Fernando Esteban Flores

"The United States themselves are essentially the greatest poem."
—Walt Whitman (the Outcasts)

Where O Walt Whitman
Bard of universal man
Blaze the democratic vistas of your vision
Where lies the largesse of the nation the simplicity of its soul
Where hides its ingenuity
Where resides its heroic hospitality
Who sings the vastness of its great psalm
Where is the man of letters where is the book
To script the scope of this great land
Only the streets grant sanctuary these days
Offer a sense of hope & openness
Better than the better life publicized
Up ahead with signs that say
We reserve the right
Denied a Bienvenida meaning
Not welcome here
Out on Frío City road Guadalupe Street
Buena Vista Commerce
Where the dark men meet
Lining the alleys
Loitering the tracks
Hunched together
American outcasts
Seeking refuge
Without direction

Home—downtown
Wherever our feet can stand
Hunger clawing at the bones
A shuffling subsistence
The city bummed
With mechanized men
Scraping out a fix among the ruts
Beneath the freeways
Littered with card box dreams
Habitués of habit addicted
To the next trumped up deal
Of empty pockets picked clean
Rummaging the garbage dumps
Of misery & regret
The doors to a rusted paradise
Of souls starved into despair
Rotting under a dead pan moon
The law of survival
Rules the place you wish
You could remember
An abstraction a blur
The Grand American expression
Poetry kosmical & bold
Folded in your wallet
Crumpled from neglect
The streets your avatar
Beckoning your return
The past a dilapidated democracy
A spoof of what you wanted
Singer of Self
You were only looking
For a way into this place
Walt Whitman

In love with the idea
Called America
Before walls
Partitioned off the land
& people became a means
To an end
Country of convenient borders
Barbed wire barricades
For those who with blood & brawn
Hoisted up the steel scaffolds of trade
The arterial lines of transport
The clanging iron riveting
The skeletal frame in place
The jackhammers breaking down stone
With blood & brow
Forever nameless faceless
Standing on the outskirts
Looking straight ahead
At a home that never was
A land where freedom rings
From a fenced in lot
Promoting a plastic posterity
On the way to the republic Walt
Words topple walls poems lessen the load we all must bear
Let us go out you & I into the barrios of this land
Our feet upon the open road

Song for America XXVIII (for Marvin Gaye)
By Fernando Esteban Flores

Nobody knows
It's absolutely so
After Lincoln
After the lynchings
After Kennedys & King
After Malcolm X & Mohammed Ali
After picket sign protest lines
After riots Civil Rights Voting Rights
After sit-ins & love-ins
marching a million miles for peace
After the horrid wars that never cease
After X number of deaths
The bans against people
Crimes against humanity
Exile & asylum
Immigration exploitation
Gun violence escalation
Mass deportations family separations
Calls for border walls & tariff wars
The entire planet a time bomb
Ticking in Times Square
Long after Marvin Gaye sang
Only love can conquer hate
The answer so absurdly clear
We learned to turn the other cheek
And in return received a deaf ear

Even those who think they do
Nobody knows

Lies bleach truth
Truth leaches lies
Facts birth fakes
Fakes sprout false things
With feathers
That cannot fly
The rich grow hip
The poor get zip
Traitors hailed patriots
Patriots acclaimed traitors
Allies enemies
Enemies allies
Haters are lovers
Lovers are haters
Zeroes the heroes
Heroes the zeroes
The White House the outhouse
E pluribus unum united in one hate
America takes its rightful place

& those who should know
Don't know a thing
Nobody knows
What's going on

De este lado del muro
By Gabriel González Núñez

Cuando me crece el pasto tanto que da pereza
dedicar un par de horas a rebanarlo todo,
entonces llamo a José, pidiéndole que venga.
Llega en su troca blanca cargada de herramientas.
Viene de manga larga, de pantalón gastado,
portando negros lentes, buscando chambear.
Se monta a su máquina revestida de verde
para dar vuelta y vuelta triturando el zacate
y dejando mi casa reluciente y muy digna.
Lo conozco muy poco. Una vez conversamos.
Me confesó que hace años que a sus padres no ve
porque ellos se quedaron del lado sur del muro.
Me dijo que sus hijos allá nunca han estado
así que no conocen ni el Sur ni a sus abuelos
(pero tienen los papeles y un día tal vez vayan).
Sólo esa vez charlamos. Él viene a trabajar.
Es decir yo le pago por cuidarme el zacate,
y como cobra poco, yo quedo siempre a gusto.

Rima infantil
By Gabriel González Núñez

Muro, murito, murero
murito separadero,
ponle fin tú al sendero
de tanto sucio viajero.
Muro, murito, murero
murito separadero,
en el mar también te espero
¡Y que frenes al balsero!

Muro, murito, murero
murito separadero,
en los aire yo te quiero
protegiendo del santero.
Muro, murito, murero
murito separadero,
no es que sea yo grosero
pero bye bye forastero.
Muro, murito, murero
murito separadero,
no es que sea yo grosero,
¡es que aquí llegué primero!

Ten Feet Higher
By Richard King Perkins II

I emailed with the Trump campaign
many times over the course of the election
freely offering the team my Midwestern insights
and slight talent of wit and words.
When Mr. Trump was out stumping
in Florida
he said that because the President of Mexico
stated that his country
would not pay for the wall
under any circumstances
the wall just got ten feet higher—
it specifically echoed
what I'd written to his advisors
a day earlier
and became my proudest literary achievement
thus far.

The Promised Wall
By Kimmy Alan

He made a promise
He kept his promise
He promised to build a wall
He promised it would be long and tall
He promised it would be big and beautiful
Made of hard concrete and cold rolled steel
He promised he'd build this wall from sea to shining sea
On this single promise he did succeed for the wall he built

My old friend
Now stands between you and me

Shelter
by Sandra Anfang

The Shell station on the corner
the most expensive one in town
charges thirty cents more than the one off the freeway.
Sometimes I spring for a tank when I get low
because I like the way it shelters squatters
compact brown men short on cash
but long on pride
in search of an honest day's work.
I tell the owner why I buy his gas
in spite of its exorbitance.
As our town dreams of a day-labor center
tries hard to raise the funds, the owner welcomes them.
I hire them when I need a hand to dig up
Agapanthus or haul away a stump
and sometimes, to inflate my tires
before the infernal machine runs out of time.
It's a gift to practice Spanish—
exercise the muscles of forgetting—
a subjunctive tense here,
an obscure adjective there.
It's my tiny contribution to the cause
like the Xmas club my mother
opened for me as a child
to fund our family's gifts.
I want to tell them to take cover.
Fears of an ICE raid
have dominated the neighborhood
airwaves for days.
I admire the way they crouch in plain sight
in tempests and in balmy weather.

I emulate the dignity of their carriage
the way they share coffee and cigarettes.

When I don't see them, I stop to ask the owner
impatient for his slow-spun response.
I want to warn them to take cover
tell them how the president abhors California
would love to purge their ranks.
I muse about the name Shell,
recall its Spanish sister, concha
which doubles as the word for womb.
How they endure
predictable as rain or drought
a small band of men hiding in plain sight
in the concha of the Shell station.

Closure
By Linda M. Crate

everyone just wants a better life
why do we resent people who are
different than us?

there is wisdom and beauty
in all cultures, if we would open
our ears and our hearts
to simply listen to someone else
and their story;

perhaps we'd learn that a fist is just
a hand that can come apart—
what could this wall
achieve?

have we not learned from berlin?
it will only serve to part
families, friends, and lovers;
it will only show to the world that we
are so arrogant as to believe
we are the only nation that matters—

diversity in this world is everywhere we look
it is beautiful, it is intriguing
we all make up the same quilt in each of our various ways
offering our talents to the world so it can be
a better place;

but this wall will only cause harm
no good could come from it
i do not understand how a wall could achieve anything
other than silence and sadness,
tears and pain;

instead of opening conversations and minds
there's a closure to communication, a closure to dreams.

more harm than good
By Linda M. Crate

there were no walls to keep out
immigrants that came to the U.S. seeking
a better life,
so why should we build walls
now?

think of the native americans robbed of their
land, of the genocide committed against
their peoples,
of all the useless death and greed against them;
these people just want a better life
why should we hold that against them?
it is sad,

but i think the american dream has been dead
for quite some time
ever since i was sixteen i have worked hard
yet i have little to show for it;

i am clothed, i have food in my apartment,
and i have clean water and a place to stay;
yet ends are barely made
the rich get richer and the poor get poorer

all the money they want to use to build this wall
could go to schools to help children who are starving
for more than simply an education,
it could go to veterans who are homeless,
and it could help so many people who are already afflicted
and suffering;

i don't understand what good a wall will do—
remember the berlin wall?
then let it fall before it becomes
because this will cause more harm than it does good.

This Just In
By Sandra Anfang

"It is better to live one day as a lion than 100 years as a sheep."
--- Mussolini, retweeted by Donald Trump

In a new twist
on an old story
Christians are feeding the masses
to the hoary Lion.
They display him as a spectacle
promenade him in the arena
like a Chimera
mousse his pompadour
into a sculpted mane
pave his throne with gilt-edged roses
build a ten-foot wall around him
to procure his safety
from the sweat of labor
the bane of blackness and Latin fever
shield him from the blood
that feeds the onion field
and greases the wheels of commerce
day after sweltering day.
From his rabid mouth
a ring of vipers spurt—
tails in each other's teeth
shooting venom
into the agape crowd.

Minions queue up behind him
feed their children--
Texas, Florida, Ohio--
to the conflagration.
He reigns supreme
a Trojan horse
whose urgent fall from grace
will loose the boots of revolution
arms of forgiveness
tools of reconstruction
gifted, palm to palm
sister to brother, father to mother
across this vast and choking land.

Walls Divide Us
By John "Jake" Cosmos Aller

In Modern America
We all live in gated communities
Trying desperately to keep them out
Out of sight
Out of mind
And out of our lives
And yet we fail
Fail to accept the others
Are human beings
Are our fellow creatures
As we wall ourselves off
Into our separate communities
We loose our humanity
And we loose our selves
As we hide in our walls
Hide in our bubbles

Mr. Trump Tear Down This Wall
By John "Jake" Cosmos Aller

Mr. Trump
Please tear down this wall
Please open up your heart
Please stop this madness
We are all Americans
We are all one people
And your wall
Will not stop us
From becoming one people
Please tear down this wall
Please build bridges to the future
Please open your heart
And let the love shine through

Walking Around
By John M. Bellinger

sometime
is the long way around
it's a weary sort of justice
how we hold on to pride
like hardtack
and questionable water
no one mentions
oases
or the history of empires
the past is an obstacle
you can always defeat
by circumnavigation
if you have the time

"A, Homeboy"
by Johnny Barboza

A, What's up Homeboy
Where you from? Huron I reply
Nah, Where you from? The Park Side
I know about Huron...I know about Park Side,I don't give a
fuck what you know….
I'm Johnny Barboza that's all you need to know.It's like
that then? It's whatever
Nothing like your first day in Juvenile Hall…
As I cry myself to sleep in Fresno.
A, What's up Homeboy
Where you from? Huron I reply
Kick it Huron...we from Avenal,
We ain't in the Valley anymore…
This is Berkeley- I pause,
And look around I see they're right,
I'm not in Huron anymore,
I'm not in Juvenile Hall anymore,
I'm about to attend UC Berkeley for
the rest of my summer. Nothing like your
First day at CHA House….
A, Homeboy where you from?
Wait I know you must be from Huron-
The Police officer smirked…
Let me see your backpack,
I don't got one I quickly answered.
You know I can take you to Juvenile Hall
If the Fast Trip manager decides to press
Charges? I don't care won't be my first time.
We know you and your friends been stealing
From this store during lunch time.

I don't have my backpack. Alright I'm taking
you to the principal's office.
The police escort my friends and I
With handcuffs, back to school and made us Walk in a
single file line as my peers
Returned from lunch. "Barboza, Barboza,
Barboza...What am I going to do with you"
Mr. Cash voice uttered into the wind.
Mr. Cash I don't know these cops don't
Like me...I don't even have my backpack.

And sure enough a Policeman hands Mr.Cash my bag. He
opens it up to find my stash of stolen
Food. "Johnny I have no choice but to suspend youu
indefinitely. Can you blame a Homeboy
For trying to get away?
Despite my unlawful youth…
I remain that Homeboy.
A person does not have to be marked
By their past. I'll always be
The Homeboy from Huron,
The Homeboy from Berkeley,
Now, I'm the homeboy who transferred from the West Hills
to the Sierra Nevadas.
Now, I'm The Homeboy who graduated from
Chico State. Now I'm the Homeboy who's telling the
young homeboys and homegirls…they can
do it to.

The Wall
By Robbi Nester

Clouds easily evade barbed wire.
Citizens of sky, we spurn your sorry efforts
to shut a people in or out, to set a border.
Subject only to the weather, we
sail above you, understand solidity
as an illusion. In time,
wire rusts. Wood grows porous,
stone swells and contracts
so often it reverts
to sand.
The roots of plants,
rivers' changing courses,
the tunneling of animals
and others
all thwart the wall.
Your barriers
are policy.
To break
their bonds is
natural law.
Everything
conspires against
your flimsy
empire.

Lament for Emma Lazarus
By Robbi Nester

I miss
America, or
what I thought
it was: a refuge,
home.
Someone has
put a padlock
on the golden door.

Ghost Wall
By Robbi Nester

After "Trespass," a photograph by Suzanne Simmons
Trees are patient, setting seed,
persisting silently. They know
what holds is what's beneath.
The roots keep spreading,
exposing veins of rebar.
At last, weather and the years
bring down the wall, insisting
this place belongs to no one.
Where the wall once was,
a stand of slender sycamores
hoist tangled branches,
rooting out the vestiges,
asserting their dominion over sky.

Wall
By Sandra Anfang

artificial
barrier
cloister
detainer
enclave
fence
garrison
hoosegow
impediment
jacket
kennel
lockup
monastery
nutshell
obstacle
penitentiary
quarantine
rampart
stockade
tenement
undercover
vault
warren
xenophobic
yoke
zero tolerance

We are Sisters!
By Patty York Raymond

We are sisters. We are one. We are born of the same fruit.

We are loved. We cherish.
We are respected. We value.
We are protected. We preserve.
We are nourished. We nurture.

Every day presents opportunities to learn, to grow, to support one another.
We are sisters. We are one. We are born of the same fruit.
We play with dolls. We learn to make friends.
We take a hike. We learn to explore.
We read our books. We learn to think.
We climb the trees. We learn we're not alone.

We are under the night sky, enveloped in a warm breeze.
We giggle with glee as trees sway softly,

encouraging our dreams.

We are sisters. We are one. We are born of the same fruit.
We want to have a career, a job in the frontier.
A home, a family, a place to call our own.
We want to make a contribution for ourselves and to others.
We want to be happy- oh, so very happy.

The passing of time makes hazy the mind. Of how we were. Of who we were.
We are sisters. We are one. We are born of the same fruit.
Our parents disagree. They don't talk.

Our parents yell. They get angry.
Our parents lose interest. They disrespect.
Our parents forget us. They turn their backs.
I go with her. You go with him.

The delicate balance of nature and nurture tips to upset on a global scale-
of what could have been and of what actually is. Each morning I see you. My reflection mirrors our

history, our culture that entwines. I used to know you. You and I had a bond but, severed like a tree

limb in a storm, it's now gone.

You and I have a past. You and I had a future- not only for you, not only for me but for you and me.

We are sisters. We are one. We are born of the same fruit.
I like to dance. You now mock my moves.
I like to sing. You now turn a deaf ear.
I like to dream of the stars. You now scoff at me.
I reach for you. You now push away from me.

The fruit rots from the trees. On my knees, I pick them off the ground. In my hands they weigh heavily.
Its juices are tears seeping through my fingers matching my own streaming down my face. I hold my
head up. I think of you not far away, and I remember that long ago tree we climbed to see people afar.

Now, people like you.

We are sisters. We are one. We are born of the same fruit.

I am not loved. I feel detached.
I am not respected. I feel distrustful.
I am not protected. I feel apprehensive.
I am not nourished. I feel deprived.

We are sisters. We are one. We are born of the same fruit.

Tinta negra
Por Xánath Caraza

Llueve en el fosforescente verde matutino.
Descubro entre la cibernética tinta negra,
entre un desconocido norte que es mi sur,
palabras entretejidas con miedos,
sentimientos disfrazados de distancia,
muros metálicos dividen dos países,
dos corazones, madres e hijos,
padres y hermanos, pasado y presente.
¿Qué nos hace diferentes?
Somos manos que escriben,
que trabajan, limpian y guían
en la oscuridad más grande.
¿Qué es una frontera?
Límites creados,
culturas forzadas
a darse la espalda.
Llueve en el fosforescente verde matutino.
Descubro entre la tinta negra
de esta pantalla de luz artificial,
los hombres y mujeres sin nombre
que apenas dejan rastro de su existencia
en los desiertos.
Anónimos seres que nunca
serán reclamados.
Esperan las madres orgullosas
a los hijos e hijas tragados por
la flamígera arena del desierto.
Rojo atardecer llena mi pantalla
y la tinta negra empieza a sangrar.

Black Ink
By Xánath Caraza
Translated by Sandra Kingery

It's raining in the phosphorescent greenness of daybreak.
I discover in the cybernetic black ink,
in an unknown north that is my south,
words interwoven with fears,
emotions disguised as distance,
metallic walls dividing two nations,
two hearts, mothers and children,
fathers and siblings, past and present.
What makes us different?
We are hands that write,
that work cleaning and guiding
in the darkest dark.
What is a border?
Created limits,
cultures forced
to turn their back.
It's raining in the phosphorescent greenness of daybreak.
I discover in the black ink
of this screen of artificial light,
nameless men and women
who barely leave a trace of their existence in the deserts.
Anonymous beings who
will never be claimed.
Proud mothers awaiting
sons and daughters swallowed
by the scorching desert sand.
Red twilight fills my screen
and the black ink begins to bleed.

Tinta Nera
Di Xánath Caraza
Tradotto da Andrea Garbin

Piore nel fosforescente verde mattutino.
Copro nella cibernetica tinta nera,
in uno sconosciuto nord che è il mio sud,
parole intrecciate con paure,
sentimenti mascherati da distanza
muri metallici dividono due paesi
due cuori, madri e figli
padri e fratelli, passato e presente.
Cosa ci rende differenti?
Siamo mani che scrivono,
che lavorano, che puliscono e guidano
nell'oscurita più gande.
Cos' è una frontiera?
Limiti creati,
culture forzate
a voltarsi le spalle.
Piove nel fosforescente verde matutino.
Scopro dentro la tinta nera di questo
schermo di luce artificiale,
le ombre e donna senza nome
che a stento lasciano una traccia della
lore esistenza nei deserti.
Esseri anonimi che non saranno
mai reclamati.
Sperano le madri orgoliose
dei loro figli e figlie inghioltiti dalla
fiammoggiante sabbia del deserto.
Il rosso crespuscolo riempie
il mio schermo e la tinta nera
cumincia a sanguinare.

What I Need Now
By Dorothy Baird

I pin labels on my lapel,
safely mark myself sympathetic.
Alone, this act inflates my ego

but not much more.
Rather, let my heart hear
the keening of wounds,

voice dissonance
with harmony of intention,
detect creeping numbness

to separating words and walls,
extend my hands to strangers,
invitation to the embrace

of an ever-widening ring.
Mend myself.
Make the circle whole.

In Concert
By Dorothy Baird

Redwoods
Shallow roots wide
Twine with others underground
Brawny network withstands tempest
In unison   Might

The Travel North
By Jose Rafael Castilleja

The heat has broken
and not in a good way.
My friends, neighbors, compatriots.
We hear your cries.

Dry to the North
No water
No shade
A perimeter
No die, no die.

Periodicos, articulos, newspapers
Todos hablan de la frontera.
Inmigrates, niños, familias
"Zero tolerance."
What a policy.?

Cartels, gangs, political asylum
They flee for a reason.

The passage way to North America
comes through South Texas.

Keep my dream Alive
By Jose Rafael Castilleja

What do I see?
It's my toe.
Why does it have a string from it?

I remember crossing a river.
My family is from El Salvador.
My daughter and I are going to *El Norte*.

Buscare trabajo
Maria will go to school.
I will send money back to *Mi tiera*.

I remember it was very HOT.
I had to carry my daughter.
She did not want to leave home
But we must.

The gangs have taken control
We had to leave.
They were going to kill ME.

It is so cold NOW.
My Maria is gone.
Keep my dream alive.

GRETEL
By Jude Brigley

In Ohio the air is so humid
that damp things turn putrid
in a hot afternoon.

Insects go about their rituals
with the concentration of priests,
as ants enter the sidewalk's labyrinth.

Nothing is simple, including a bus –
Ride for shopping for sustenance;
the peppers are too large
and the labels too unfamiliar.

Perhaps, Columbus is a woman
who in the morning sunlight
emerges as past her prime,
though touched up with
a splash of new clothes.

Or maybe Columbus
is the tramp in the municipal
park, his trolley filled with
tawdry rubbish, half sleeping

in the sunlight but dangerous
as a snake. watching children
play through dead eyes.

In this city everything
is distorted - time

memory and the reasons
why you came to such a place:
where the safety of bread
and vigilance keep
eyes on the emerging track.

WHERE HAVE ALL THE FLOWERS GONE
By Jude Brigley

The Kingston trio are on the radio.

        The bells are calling from St Michael's

as the sun seeps through the curtains,
                        lighting
up the dusty bedroom,

      with its election victory cuttings pasted on the
unpainted door.

Below her the kitchen bustles with breakfast

        and argument.

Her grandmother is calling

but she snuggles into cold sheets,
                    ignoring potato
peeling duties.

Her mind returns to earlier times

when the world seemed to be a changing

>   not a needle stuck repeating itself
>   revolving in its old groove.

Instead she savours her father's music and is surprised to
find tears in her eyes
as she sings out sings out *A hundred miles, a hundred miles*
Sad as blind windows on a shadowed street.

CROSSINGS
By Jude Brigley

So many made the trek

        in groaning wooden boxes,

crossing   the   ocean

        with only a song in the heart,
                in a tongue learnt
far away and
                used in the heart
                  of the house as
children forget

the old ways.

                Here, in the hot heat of
Ohio's summer

                the Irish come to tell
their stories,

  drink their dark brew,
            bang their drums.

            This pocket handkerchief of
parkland

becomes emerald.   But voices betray

        the American drawl of betrothings.

They shed a tear
    for a past they never knew

and if they had, they too would have risked all

on that   ocean

with   bitter hope

and   happy regret.

Traductoras al griego: Traducido por el curso de literatura española e hispanoamericana del Instituto Cervantes de Atenas dirigido por la profesora: María José Martínez Rodríguez. Alumnas y traductoras: Angelikí Patera, Stella Panagopoulou, Katerina Apostolaki, Varvara Asouti, Tatiana Basakou, Timoklia Dougali, Afroditi Papatheodorou.

Traductora al inglés: Sandra Kingery

Nuestros niños
Por Xánath Caraza

Si es uno, diez mil
o mil quinientos los perdidos,
el dolor es el mismo,
la indignación aún mayor.

No hay canciones de cuna
a quien susurrar por las noches,
las camas están vacías.

Ni a quien cobijar en las tardes frías,
las casas están incompletas.
No hay fuego en el hogar.

Una generación adolorida.
No hay cuerpos que abrazar.

Niño mío, en la oscuridad te vislumbro.
Niña mía, en las garras de la maldad estás.

¿Cómo alcanzar tus pequeñas manos?
¿Cómo calmar tu sed?
¿Cómo sentir tu aroma?
¿Cómo escuchar tu dulce voz?

¿Quién consolará tu hermosa alma?
¿Tendrás qué comer?
¿Quién dirá tu nombre con ternura?
¿Quién rezará por ti con amor?

Y, ¿en las noches de tormenta?

Niño mío, niña mía,

¿cómo sabrás que sigo junto a ti?

Atenas, Grecia, 13 de junio de 2018.

Δικά μας παιδιά.

Αν ένα είναι,δέκα χιλιάδες
η χίλια πεντακόσια τα χαμένα
ο πόνος είναι ο ίδιος
η αγανάκτηση ακόμα μεγαλύτερη.

Δεν έχω σε ποιόν να μουρμουρίσω
νανουρίσματα τις νύχτες,
τα κρεβάτια αδειανά.

Ούτε ποιόν να σκεπάσω τα κρύα απογεύματα,
τα σπίτια είναι γκρεμισμένα,ανοκλήρωτα.
Δεν υπάρχει φωτιά στην εστία.

Μια γενιά πονεμένη.
Δεν υπάρχουν κορμιά να αγκαλιάσω.

Αγόρι μου, μέσα στην σκοτεινιά σε διακρίνω.
Κορίτσι μου, στα γαμψά νύχια της κακότητας βρίσκεσαι.

Πώς να φτάσω τα μικρά σου χέρια;
Πώς να σβήσω τη δίψα σου;
Πώς να νοιώσω το αρωμά σου;
Πώς να ακούσω την γλυκιά σου φωνή;

Ποιος θα παρηγορήσει την όμορφη ψυχή σου;
Θάχεις τι να φας;
Ποιος θα πει το όνομά σου με τρυφεράδα;
Ποιος θα προσευχηθεί για σένα με αγάπη;

Και τις νύχτες με καταιγίδα;

Αγόρι μου, κορίτσι μου;

Πως θα μάθεις πως είμαι πάντα μαζί σου;

Αθήνα, Ελλάδα, 13 Ιουνίου 2018.

Our Sons and Daughters

If it is one, ten thousand
or fifteen hundred who are lost,
the pain is the same,
the indignation even greater.

There are no lullabies
to murmur at night,
the beds are vacant.

No one to bundle up on cold afternoons,
the houses are incomplete.
There is no fire in the hearth.

A generation grieving.
No bodies to embrace.

My son, I perceive you through the dark.
My daughter, malevolent claws constrain you.

How do I reach your little hands?
How do I quench your thirst?
How do I find your scent?
How do I hear your sweet voice?

Who will calm your beautiful soul?
Is there anything for you to eat?
Who will say your name with tenderness?
Who will pray for you with love?

And, during stormy nights,

My son, my daughter,

how will you know that I am still by your side?

Athens, Greece, 13 June 2018.

Contributor Bios

(In order of appearance)

Hector Luis Alamo is a Chicago writer now floating on the edge of Las Vegas, Hector Alamo is the editor and publisher of Enclave. He is the former deputy editor for Latino Rebels, as well as the former managing editor for Gozamos, a Latino 'artivist' site based in his hometown. He has contributed to RedEye, a Chicago daily geared toward millennials, and La Respuesta, a New York-based site for the Puerto Rican Diaspora, plus a number of publications, including the Huffington Post. He studied history at the University of Illinois-Chicago, where his focus was on ethnic relations in the United States.

Jill Evans, also known as Jill Evans Petzall, makes documentary films, media art installations, writes poetry and essays, and teaches about social justice from a female perspective. She is the winner of four Emmy Awards for her scripts and documentary films. She lives in St. Louis, MO, and started her career in her 40s while raising three young children as a single mother. All her work is fueled by a graduate degree in Philosophy. Now in her 70s, she has just begun to publish the poetry that she has been writing all her life. She writes poetry to hold life still enough so she can finally figure it out.

Roger Sippl studied creative writing at the University of California at Irvine, the University of California at Berkeley (including a class with Thom Gunn) and at Stanford Continuing Studies. He has published poetry in the Ocean State Review and over a dozen other literary journals and anthologies. He has also published in JAMA Oncology and CHEST, which are actually medical journals.

While a student at UC Berkeley in the 1970's, Sippl was diagnosed with Stage IIIB Hodgkin's Lymphoma, which was treated aggressively with surgery, radiation therapy and chemotherapy, allowing him to live relapse-free to this day.

See more poetry and photos on his website at:
www.rogersippl.com

Seres Jaime Magaña was born in Guadalajara, Jalisco, Mexico. He has been published in several anthologies, including the Raving Press' Bad Hombres and Nasty Women which features his work The People United. His latest publication Agua Dulce appears in Rio Grande Valley Boundless Anthology of 2018. He is the author of the bilingual play The Tragic Corrido of Romeo and Lupe, performed at the Pharr Community Theater, and is host for Saturday Open Mic Night at Luna Coffee House, and Mac Nites at Yerberia Cultura.

C. R. Resetarits has had work recently in Litro and Chicago Quarterly Review; out now in Chattahoochee Review and Confrontation; out soon in So to Speak and December. She has been nominated twice for a Pushcart Prize, 2016 & 2017. Her poetry collection, BROOD, was published by Mongrel Empire Press in 2015. She lives in Faulkner-riddled Oxford, Mississippi.
crresetarits.wordpress.com
crresetarits.tumblr.com/

Laurie Jurs: My name is Laurie Jurs. I live in Arizona, 40 miles north of Nogales, which straddles the Mexican border, and have for 34 years. This poem is about the murder of Jose Antonio Elena Rodriguez in 2012. He was sixteen years old. In order to shoot into Mexico, the U.S. Border Patrol agent had to step up to the wall and shoot through the slats. The agent shot down a steep cliff onto Calle International, which is right below the Wall. The agent was acquitted of second degree murder but will be re-tried on manslaughter charges this year. The Wall does not stop people nor does it stop bullets.

Kristin Barendsen is a Santa Fe writer whose work has appeared in *The Sun, American Poet, Nailed, Gravel, Atticus Review,* and many other venues. Awards include the Academy of American Poets Prize and two Southwest Writers awards. She is co-author of *Photography: New Mexico* and a former contributing editor of *Yoga Journal*.

Catherine Lee founded and ran for 13 years Studio Red Top, Inc., a loft space/nonprofit in Boston where she produced concerts, jam sessions, and readings. Lee also began exploring poetry as a percussive voice with jazz musicians—including joint gigs with her mentor, Beat poet/hipster tedjoans in 1986-87. Ted shared his "Jazz is my religion" philosophy, and Lee was inspired to carry this legacy forward. Today, from San Antonio TX and Asheville NC, Lee reads as a soloist at poetry events or with improvising musicians when sitting in "on poem." Some of her multimedia pieces are archived on Soundcloud (http://soundcloud.com/jazz-cat-lee) and Vimeo (http://vimeo.com/jazzovation). Lee has produced radio specials about jazz poetry and created several artist handmade, signed, numbered, limited edition chapbooks augmented with music. She also blogs about notable musical/poetic collaborations on her Facebook page, Jazz Ovation Inn.

Richard Nester has twice been a fellow of the Fine Arts Work Center in Provincetown. He has published essays on social justice topics in The Catholic Agitator, a publication of the Los Angeles Catholic Worker, and poetry in numerous magazines, including Ploughshares, Seneca Review, and Callaloo and on-line in The Cortland Review, Qarrtsiluni and Inlandia. He has two collections of poetry, Buffalo Laughter and Gunpowder Summers, both published by Kelsay Books.

Rick Blum has been chronicling life's vagaries-- often with a humorous spin -- through essays and poetry for more than 25 years during stints as a nightclub owner, high-tech manager, market research mogul, and, most recently, old geezer. His writings have appeared in *The Literary Hatchet, The Satirist*, and *The Moon Magazine*, among others. He is also a frequent contributor to the *Humor Times*, and has been published in numerous poetry anthologies. Mr. Blum is a three-time winner of the annual Carlisle Poetry Contest. His poem, *Tomfoolery*, received honorable mention in *The Boston Globe* Deflategate poetry challenge. Currently, he is holed up in his Massachusetts office trying to pen the perfect bio, which he plans to share as soon as he stops laughing at the sheer futility of this effort.

Michael Garrigan lives in Pennsylvania where he writes and teaches high school English. His essays and poetry have previously appeared in publications such as *Gray's Sporting Journal, The Drake Magazine,* and *San Pedro River Review.* You can find more of his writing at www.raftmanspath.com.

Sammy Ybarra: I am Sammy Ybarra, born/raised in San Diego, a chicano from Logan Heights. My mother, Sofia Erminia Gonzalez Ybarra, one of 14 children to Juan DeDios Gonzalez and Cruz Romero, was the only High School graduate of her 14 brothers and sisters. I attended Our Lady of Guadalupe Parochial School, St Judes Academy, St Michaels Academy and St Augustine High School.

Besides 17 years with The County of San Diego, several years with Diego and Son Printing and an Associate at Wal Mart and The Home Depot, i worked 11 years in the office of U S Senator Barbara Boxer as her Community Representative for San Diego, Riverside and Imperial Counties.

My 45 years of work diversity has given me a unique experience perspective that allows me to see and feel a broad range of issues as well as a difference of opinion. That two of my three older brothers are Harvard graduates only gives me that much more insight and that my nephews and nieces) from my brother Richard Ybarra) are the grand children of our late brother and union Leader Cesar Chavez..

For the past 40 plus years i have been a singer, song writer, entertainer with over 30 years of performing throughout the greater San Diego area as well as Hawaii, southwest United States singing with bands from Funk top 40 music as well as Latin Groups .. and in Mexico.... where i was singing with Mariachi Mexicano de Frank Vialba.

I have been writing poetry now for just a few years and i acknowledge that although im still a new writer with so much to learn, i pride myself that i have written some 180 plus poems in just this past year and a half.

Miranda Rocha is a computer repair tech turned poet. She prefers metaphors and similes to RAM and processors. She comes from Mission, Texas and is a friend to any Lechusa or Chupacabra that she may encounter. Miranda focuses on straightforward honesty and disturbing societal cues.

Sunayna Pal: Born and raised in Mumbai, India, Sunayna Pal moved to the US after her marriage. A double postgraduate from XLRI and Annamalai University, she worked in the corporate world for five odd years before opting out to embark on her heart's pursuits - Raising funds for NGOs by selling quilled art and became a certified handwriting analyst. Now, a new mother, she devotes all her free time to writing and Heartfulness. Dozens of her articles and poems have been published and she is a proud contributor of many international anthologies. Her name has recently appeared in "Subterranean Blue Poetry," "Cecile's Writers" and "Poetry Super highway" She is part of an anthology that is about to break the Guinness world of records. Know more on sunaynapal.com

Anna Fores Tamayo: Being an academic not paid enough for my trouble, I wanted instead to do something that mattered: work with asylum seekers. I advocate for marginalized refugee families from Mexico and Central America.

Working with asylum seekers is heart wrenching, yet satisfying. It is also quite humbling.

My labor has eased my own sense of displacement, being a child refugee, always trying to find home. In parallel, poetry is the hidden side I don't often let others see, though lately, this has changed. I have published in *The Raving Press, Acentos Review, Rigorous, Frontera*-- an international literary magazine from Spain -- *Indolent Books, Chaleur Magazine,* and most recently, *Memoir.* My poetry will also be included in the *Laurel Review* and an anthology published by *Cosmographia Books* in late 2018, as well as another anthology, *Detained Voices/Voces detenidas* with my poem "Elegy to a Refugee Girl / Oda a una niña refugiada." Lastly, I have photography published in *Acentos Review* and *The Bozalta Collective*. A digital rendition of my poems "Refugee / Refugiado," featuring my own photography, whose English version first appeared in *The Raving Press,* was published in UC Davis' "Humanizing Deportation."

I hope you like my latest piece, a modern sonnet, written simultaneously in both languages. I am not sure when I wrote one language or the other... I just know that writing — in either language — is a catharsis from the cruelty yet ecstasy of my work.

Wendy Baron is a semi-retired nurse and social worker who has loved poetry from a young age. Her work has appeared in both Blue Hole, and The Enigmatist. She is a member of the Sun Poet Society in San Antonio, Texas, and has volunteered with programs that help migrants and which promote social equity.

Natalie D-Napoleon was raised on a farm on the outskirts of Fremantle, Western Australia with her three siblings by Croatian-immigrant parents. For 20 plus years she toured and performed as a singer-songwriter playing shows across Australia, Europe and the United States. She holds an MA in Writing from Swinburne University and works as a Writing Center Coordinator at a California City College. She has had creative non-fiction and poetry published in Entropy, Westerly, Australian Poetry Journal, Hippocampus, and Writer's Digest, including a recent publication in Larry Smith's *The Best Advice in Six Words*, alongside Elizabeth Gilbert and Madeleine Albright. She is a two-time finalist for the Penelope Niven Creative Nonfiction Award at the 2018 and 2017 International Literary Awards. Her poem "First Blood: A Sestina" recently won the prestigious Bruce Dawe Poetry Prize through the University of Southern Queensland, Australia.

Twitter and Instagram: @nataliednapo
Website: www.nataliednapoleon.org

Octavio Quintanilla is the author of the poetry collection, If I Go Missing (Slough Press, 2014) and the 2018-2020 Poet Laureate of San Antonio, TX. His poetry, fiction, translations, and photography have appeared, or are forthcoming, in journals such as Salamander, RHINO, Alaska Quarterly Review, Pilgrimage, Green Mountains Review, Southwestern American Literature, The Texas Observer, Existere: A Journal of Art & Literature, and elsewhere. Reviews of his work can be found at CutBank Literary Journal, Concho River Review, San Antonio Express-News, American Microreviews & Interviews, Southwestern American Literature, Pleiades, and others. You can check out his visual poems in Gold Wake Live, Newfound, Chachalaca Review, Chair Poetry Evenings, and Twisted Vine Literary Arts Journal. Visual poems are forthcoming in Red Wedge Journal and in The American Journal of Poetry. He holds a Ph.D. from the University of North Texas and is the regional editor for Texas Books in Review. He teaches Literature and Creative Writing in the M.A./M.F.A. program at Our Lady of the Lake University in San Antonio, Texas. Find him on Instagram @writeroctavioquintanilla & Twitter @OctQuintanilla

Teri Garcia Ruiz is a Texas native who enjoys both reading and writing poetry.

Steven Alvarez is the author of *The Codex Mojaodicus*, winner of the 2016 Fence Modern Poets Prize. He has also authored the novels in verse *The Pocho Codex* (2011) and *The Xicano Genome* (2013), both published by Editorial Paroxismo, and the chapbooks, *Tonalamatl, El Segundo's Dream Notes* (2017, Letter [r] Press), *Un/documented, Kentucky* (2016, winner of the Rusty Toque Chapbook Prize), and *Six Poems from the Codex Mojaodicus* (2014, winner of the Seven Kitchens Press Rane Arroyo Poetry Prize). His work has appeared in the *Best Experimental Writing* (BAX), *Berkeley Poetry Review*, *Fence*, *Huizache*, *The Offing*, and *Waxwing*. Follow Steven on Instagram @stevenpaulalvarez and Twitter @chastitellez.

Vanessa Caraveo has been avidly involved in writing throughout the years and was published in HWG's, "Out of Many One: Celebrating Diversity," 2017 anthology, had her winning essays published for the IMIA for two consecutive years in a row (2013 and 2014) and also has various fiction, non-fiction and poems published for diverse organizations. She has been a volunteer and member for many non-profit groups and emphasizes the importance of making a positive difference and hopes to uplift the lives of others through her literary work.

Sharon Lundy was born and raised in San Antonio, Texas. She has a B.A. in Communication Arts from The University of the Incarnate Word. She is an active member of Voces Cosmicas, a diverse group of San Antonio poets and The San Antonio Screenwriter's Guild. Sharon is currently working on her first chapbook titled "Train Up A Child" which is a bittersweet, cautionary guide for her two sons Langston and Ellington.

Sheena Pillai Singh is an Engineer by Profession, working with an Infrastructure Company in New Delhi, India. Writing is my passion which I am pursuing since my University Days. A few of my poems were published in wall magazines, portals and blogs. I write to relieve stress, or when I am at peace or when I sight an object of my interest. My other passion involves Tarot reading, Crystal Healing and Spiritual cleansing.

Fernando Esteban Flores graduated from the University of Texas at Austin with a B.A. In English. He taught writing at several secondary schools in San Antonio and received 2 ExCEL awards for excellence in teaching from KENS 5-TV, and was chosen as a distinguished educator from Bexar County by Trinity University's Trinity Prize Committee. His work has appeared in: the San Antonio Express-News, Voices de la Luna, The Americas Review, The Texas Observer, The Thing Itself Journal (Our Lady of the Lake University), rogueagent journal (issue 25), Written with a Spoon: a Poet's Cookbook, Is This Forever or What?, Lost Children of the River, (The Raving Press), writersofthe riogrande.com and was nominated for a Pushcart Prize in poetry. His three books of poetry: Ragged Borders, Red Accordion Blues & BloodSongs are available from Hijo del Sol Publishing and were recently archived at the Ozuna Learning Center & Library at Palo Alto College.
Visit his webpage: www.madwarbler.com

Gabriel González Núñez, uruguayo, vive en Brownsville, Texas. Es docente de la Universidad de Texas en el Valle del

Río Grande, donde forma traductores e intérpretes. Ha publicado cuentos y microcuentos en las revistas La Marca Hispánica, Ventana Abierta, Círculo, Entre Líneas, Narrativas, Punto en Línea, Tiempos Oscuros, miNatura, El Narratorio y The Chachalaca Review. Fue galardonado con el Premio Platero 2012 en la categoría cuento. Recibió el segundo accésit del Premio Enrique Labrador Ruiz 2009 y mención de honor en el 36o Concurso Doctor Alberto Manini Ríos. También fue finalista del X Concurso Literario Gonzalo Rojas Pizarro. Asimismo, ha publicado poesía en la revista La Marca Hispánica, en la antología Boundless 2017 y en el blog La Bloga. Lleva un blog literario en GabrielGonzalezNunez.wordpress.com.

Richard King Perkins II is a state-sponsored advocate for residents in long-term care facilities. He lives in Crystal Lake, IL, USA with his wife, Vickie and daughter, Sage. He is a three-time Pushcart, Best of the Net and Best of the Web nominee whose work has appeared in more than fifteen hundred publications.

Kimmy Alan is a wannabe poet from the land of Lake Woebegone. A retired steel worker who was diagnosed with stage 4 cancer, Kimmy Alan pursed his love of poetry as a distraction while undergoing chemo and radiation. For him, poetry has proven to be a powerful catharsis as he is currently in remission. When he isn't writing he spends time with his four wonderful nieces, whom he says "are driving him to pieces."

Sandra Anfang is a Northern California teacher, poet, and visual artist. She is the author of four poetry collections and several chapbooks. Her poems have appeared in numerous journals, including *Poetalk, San Francisco Peace and Hope, Unbroken Literary Journal, Rattle,* and *Spillway.* Her chapbook, **Looking Glass Heart,** was published by Finishing Line Press in early 2016. **Road Worrier: Poems of the Inner and Outer Landscape**, was released in April of this year from the same publisher, and a full-length collection, **Xylem Highway**, is forthcoming from Main Street Rag. She was nominated for a Best Short Fictions award in 2016 and more recently, for a Pushcart Prize. Sandra is founder and host of the monthly poetry series, Rivertown Poets, in Petaluma, and a California Poet/Teacher in the Schools. To write, for her, is to breathe.

Linda M. Crate is a Pennsylvanian native born in Pittsburgh yet raised in the rural town of Conneautville. Her poetry, short stories, articles, and reviews have been published in a myriad of magazines both online and in print. She has five published chapbooks A Mermaid *Crashing Into Dawn* (Fowlpox Press - June 2013), *Less Than A Man* (The Camel Saloon - January 2014), *If Tomorrow Never Comes* (Scars Publications, August 2016), *My Wings Were Made to Fly* (Flutter Press, September 2017), and *splintered with terror* (Scars Publications, January 2018).

John ("Jake") Cosmos Aller is a novelist, poet, and former Foreign Service officer having served 27 years with the U.S. State Department serving in ten countries (Korea, Thailand, India, the Eastern Caribbean (lived in Barbados

but covering Antigua, Barbados, Dominica, Grenada, St Kitts, St Lucia, and St Vincent) and Spain. Prior to joining the U.S. State Department, Jake taught overseas for eight years. Jake served in the Peace Corps in Korea. He grew up in Berkeley but has lived in Seattle, Stockton, Washington DC, Alexandria, Virginia and Medford, Oregon. He has traveled to over 45 countries and 49 states. He has been writing poetry, fiction, and novels for years. He has completed four SF novels and is seeking publication. His work has appeared in numerous literary magazines online. His poetry blog can be found at
https://theworldaccordingtocosmos.com

John M. Bellinger is from East Syracuse, NY.

He has been an editor for a long-serving Poetry Journal for over 25 years..

This would not be his first published work.

Circumstances permitting, it will not be his last.

Johnny Barboza: I grew up in Huron, California in the heart of the Central Valley. It is a very rural community and agricultural based full of migrant farmworkers. I graduated high school and went on to attend junior college in northern California. From Butte College I transferred to Chico State where I received a Bachelor's in English Education and minor in Creative Writing. I identify myself as Chicano and produce work which reflects my Mexican upbringing.

Robbi Nester is a first generation American whose grandmother fled Russian pogroms at the beginning of the 20th century. She is the author of three books of poems—a chapbook, Balance (White Violet, 2012), and two collections of Poetry, A Likely Story (Moontide, 2014) and Other-Wise (Kelsey, 2017). Her third collection, Narrow Bridge, will be published by Main Street Rag. She has edited two anthologies: The Liberal Media Made Me Do It! (Nine Toes, 2014) and an Ekphrastic ebook, Over the Moon: Birds, Beasts, and Trees—celebrating the photography of Beth Moon (available to read at http://www.poemeleon.org/over-the-moon-birds-Beasts-and).

Patty York Raymond is a Multi-Award Winning Children's Book Author and native Texan. Her interactive children's books, It's Too Windy! and The ABCs to Ranching along with their corresponding original theme songs 'That's What My Grandma Said' and 'Take Me To The Ranch,' have been honored by The Texas Authors Association and the International Latino Book Awards. Patty earned her M.Ed. in Early Childhood Education from the University of Houston and her Administration and Supervision from Texas A&M International University. Patty York Raymond has enjoyed working with children, families, and educators in a variety of roles including social worker, bilingual teacher and administrator. She especially enjoys visiting elementary schools throughout Texas and beyond to share her stories and encourage students to read and write. She and her family reside in South Texas where she is an independent education consultant as well as owner/director of Abrazo Case Management Services for Children and Pregnant Women. Patty can be contacted for school visits at pattyraymondbooks@gmail.com.

Xánath Caraza is a traveler, educator, poet and short story writer. She writes for La Bloga, Smithsonian Latino Center, Seattle Escribe and Revista Literaria Monolito. For the 2018 International Latino Book Awards, she received First Place for Lágrima roja and Sin preámbulos/Without Preamble for "Best Book of Poetry in Spanish" and "Best Book Bilingual Poetry". Syllables of Wind received the 2015 International Book Award for Poetry. Her books of verse Where the Light is Violet, Black Ink, Ocelocíhuatl, Conjuro and her book of short fiction What the Tide Brings have won national and international recognition. Her other books of poetry are Hudson, Le sillabe del vento, Noche de colibríes, Corazón pintado, and her second short story collection, Metztli.

Dorothy Baird: Dorothy Baird 's work appears in her chapbook Indelible Ripples (Aldrich Press) and in such journals and anthologies as Kakalak, Iodine, Rose in the World, Into the Coastal Sun, County Lines, and New Verse News. She taught in the English Department of Western Connecticut University and was a managing editor for Hitchcock Press. Though born and raised in Texas, she calls herself a corporate tramp, having zigzagged across the country with her family. She is now at home in Chapel Hill, North Carolina.

Jose Rafael Castilleja is a writer, poet, engineer, and community leader. He has written technical articles and descriptions of local events for a local newspaper. He was born and raised in the Rio Grande Valley in Texas.

Jude Brigley has been a teacher, an editor, a coach and a performance poet. She is now writing more for the page. Attachments area

Gabriel Hugo Sanchez is the founder and chief editor at The Raving Press. Gabriel is also an author under the pen name Gabriel Hugo, with his most recent publication titled Tenochtitlan Must Fall (book 1, The X Series). For more, visit http://gabrielhugo.com/

About The Raving Press

The Raving Press has been publishing anthologies and chapbooiks since 1998 in the Rio Grande Valley in South Texas, one of the most dynamic and highly energized centers of the U.S.-Mexico border. We enjoy the most financially, commercially, artistically, and culturaly rich traditions and lifestyles. The Rio Grande Valley is the next Constantinople, the next Rome, the next New York, or the next Tenochtitlan; a jewel and a wonder of the world. For more about what is taking place in the magical Valley, visit www.theravingpress.com.

www.ingramcontent.com/pod-product-compliance
Lightning Source LLC
Chambersburg PA
CBHW030939090426
42737CB00007B/474